A TRUE BOOK™

# The Seven Continents

# Australia and Oceania

BARBARA A. SOMERVILL

**Children's Press®**
An Imprint of Scholastic Inc.

**Content Consultant**
Frank Bongiorno, Ph.D., Academic Professor
School of History, Australian National University

Library of Congress Cataloging-in-Publication Data
Names: Somervill, Barbara A., author.
Title: Australia and Oceania / by Barbara A. Somervill.
Description: New York, NY : Children's Press, an imprint of Scholastic Inc. , 2019. | Series: A true book |
    Includes bibliographical references and index.
Identifiers: LCCN 2018024808| ISBN 9780531128077 (library binding) | ISBN 9780531134153 (pbk.)
Subjects: LCSH: Australia—Juvenile literature. | Oceania—Juvenile literature.
Classification: LCC DU96 .S664 2019 | DDC 994—dc23
LC record available at https://lccn.loc.gov/2018024808

All rights reserved. Published in 2019 by Children's Press, an imprint of Scholastic Inc.
Printed in North Mankato, MN, USA 113

SCHOLASTIC, CHILDREN'S PRESS, A TRUE BOOK™, and associated logos are trademarks and/or registered trademarks of Scholastic Inc.

Scholastic Inc., 557 Broadway, New York, NY 10012

1 2 3 4 5 6 7 8 9 10 R 28 27 26 25 24 23 22 21 20 19

**Front: Australia and Oceania**
**Back: Great white shark**

# Find the Truth!

**Everything** you are about to read is true *except* for one of the sentences on this page.

## Which one is **TRUE**?

**T or F**  People have lived in Australia for about 65,000 years.

**T or F**  All the islands of Oceania are volcanic islands.

Find the answers in this book.

# Contents

THE **BIG** TRUTH!

## Ocean Acidification

Parrotfish

The Pinnacles in Australia's Nambung National Park

Ferdinand Magellan

Note: Some geographers consider the entire
island of New Guinea as a part of Oceania.

New Guinea

ASIA

TUVALU

PAPUA
NEW
GUINEA

SOLOMON ISLANDS

Timor Sea

Coral
Sea

VANUATU

NEW CALEDONIA
(France)

FIJI

Northern
Territory

Queensland

AUSTRALIA

Western
Australia

South
Australia

Darling River

New
South
Wales

INDIAN
OCEAN

PACIFIC
OCEAN

Great
Australian
Bight

Murray R.

Canberra

Victoria

NEW
ZEALAND

Tasman
Sea

Wellington

Chatham

Tasmania

N

W E

S

N MARIANA IS. (U.S.)

MARSHALL
ISLANDS

Hawaii

0       500 MI

PALAU

GUAM
(U.S.)

MICRONESIA

0       800 KM

NAURU

KIRIBATI

Equator

SOLOMON IS.

TOKELAU

N

PAPUA
NEW
GUINEA

TUVALU

WALLIS &
FUTUNA
(France)

SAMOA

AMERICAN SAMOA (U.S.)

VANUATU

COOK IS. (N.Z.)

FIJI

FRENCH
POLYNESIA
(France)

AUSTRALIA

NEW
CALEDONIA
(France)

TONGA

Tonga

PITCAIRN
(U.K.)

Antarctic Circle

NEW ZEALAND

ANTARCTICA

6

# Continent Close-up

**Australia and Oceania do not cover much land.**
Together, they are smaller than any other continent. However, they span a huge part of the globe, with islands spread throughout much of the Pacific Ocean. Some of these islands, such as Australia, are very large, while others are quite small.

**New Zealand**

| | |
|---|---|
| **Land area** | 3,291,903 square miles (8,525,990 sq km) |
| **Number of independent countries** | 14 |
| **Estimated population (2018)** | 41,183,198 |
| **Main languages** | English, French, Maori (New Zealand), Tok Pisin (Papua New Guinea), and hundreds of other native languages of islanders and Aboriginal people |
| **Largest country** | Australia |
| **Smallest country** | Nauru |
| **Fast fact** | Australia and Oceania take up 5.3 percent of Earth's land. |

Atolls such as Caroline
Island are rings of coral
with a lagoon in the center.

Oceania is a large ocean region that
contains thousands of islands

# CHAPTER 1

# Land and Climate

Australia and Oceania contain some of the oldest land on Earth—and some of the newest. Australia has surface land that is 4.4 billion years old. New land on volcanic islands, such as New Zealand and Vanuatu, is formed with every eruption. In the Pacific Ocean, rings of coral islands called atolls rise above the ocean's surface. Ocean waves break down the coral to form new islands.

# All Kinds of Islands

An archipelago is a group of islands arranged in a string. Fiji, the Marshalls, Kiribati, the Solomons, Vanuatu, and Tonga are archipelagos in Oceania. Some archipelagos were formed from volcanic eruptions. Others, such as Tuvalu and Nauru, are atolls. At a size of just 8.1 square miles (21 sq km), Nauru is also one of the world's smallest countries!

| ISLANDS IN AN ARCHIPELAGO | | | | | | | | | | |
|---|---|---|---|---|---|---|---|---|---|---|
| Archipelago Island | Fiji | Micronesia | Vanuatu | Solomon Islands | Palau | Marshall Islands | Tuvalu | Kiribati | Tonga | Samoa |
| Number of Islands | 300 | 600 | 83 | 900+ | 258 | 34 | 9 | 33 | 170 | 9 |

The beautiful white sand beaches of Oceania are made of parrotfish poop! Parrotfish eat coral and poop sand.

# Volcanic Peaks

Papua New Guinea, Fiji, Vanuatu, and New Zealand feature Oceania's highest volcanic peaks. At 14,793 feet (4,509 meters), Papua New Guinea's Mount

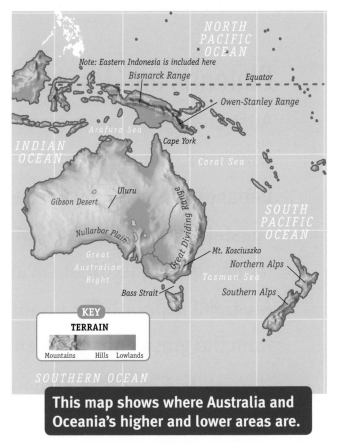

**This map shows where Australia and Oceania's higher and lower areas are.**

Wilhelm is the tallest of all. Oceania's volcanoes lie along the Ring of Fire, a series of volcanoes circling the Pacific Ocean. In 2018, eruptions occurred at Ambae in Vanuatu and at Kadovar and Bagana in Papua New Guinea. Active volcanoes present serious danger, and people living near Ambae had to leave their homes to stay safe.

# Plateaus and Plains

Australia and Oceania make up Earth's flattest continent. The island of Australia is a mix of flatlands, deserts, grass-covered plains, sandy coastal plains, and raised **plateaus**. The low mountains of the Great Dividing Range in eastern Australia separate the populated eastern plains from the grasslands and central deserts. Papua New Guinea and New Zealand are mountainous, while the islands of Oceania are either high volcanoes or flat atolls.

The Pinnacles are a breathtaking series of limestone formations in Western Australia's Nambung National Park.

## Linked by Water

The nations within the continent are linked not by land, but by water. For centuries, people traveled between the islands of the Pacific Ocean by ocean-going canoes. The Indian Ocean curls around Australia's west coast. From the Marshall Islands to New Zealand, shallow seas surround the island nations. The Timor, Arafura, Coral, and Tasman Seas all lie along the Australian coast.

People seek shelter from a rainstorm in Tuvalu.

# Climate

In much of Australia and New Zealand, there are four different seasons, with hot summers, mild spring and fall weather, and cold winters. Areas near the equator, such as Palau, Samoa, and Tuvalu, have little temperature change throughout the year. They also get a lot of rain. For example, Micronesia receives 187 inches (475 centimeters) yearly! Seasons in the Southern **Hemisphere** are opposite to those above the equator. January is the best time to head for the beach, while snow can fall in July.

# A Natural Wonder: Uluru

Uluru is a massive monolith, or single piece of stone. The rock rises 1,142 feet (348 m) out of the ground. It is 2.2 miles (3.6 km) long and 1.5 miles (2.4 km) wide. For thousands of years, Australia's Anangu people have held Uluru as a sacred location. They have recorded their long history through paintings around the base of the rock. Uluru is an Australian national treasure, a United Nations World Heritage Area, and the largest single monolith on Earth.

Uluru is located within Uluru-Kata Tjuṯa National Park, in Australia's Northern Territory.

Osprey Reef is located off the northeastern coast of Australia.

Coral reefs like this one form the base for many atolls in Australia and Oceania.

# CHAPTER 2

# Plants and Animals

A biome is a natural area known for a certain climate, landscape, and living things. A wide range of remarkable insects, plants, reptiles, birds, fish, and **marsupials** live in the varied biomes of Australia and Oceania. Many species are found nowhere else on Earth. Some, such as koalas and wombats, are cute and can even be friendly. But the continent is also home to many deadly critters, including stonefish, sea krait snakes, taipan snakes, funnel web spiders, Australian box jellies, and saltwater crocodiles.

Thorny devils are covered in spikes that help discourage predators from eating them.

# Deserts

Deserts are rare in Oceania but quite common in Australia. The largest is the Great Victoria Desert, and the smallest is the Pedirka Desert. Australia's deserts host many reptiles, including goannas, skinks, and thorny devils. Short plants such as wattles, saltbrush, and Sturt's desert peas grow above underground springs.

In New Zealand, the Rangipo Desert gets 78 inches (198 cm) of rain yearly but no plant growth. Rangipo's soil is volcanic and does not hold water.

# Trees Along the Mountainsides

The mountains of Fiji and New Zealand are heavily covered with temperate forests. Common trees include beeches and evergreens. New Zealand's mountains are higher and colder. They feature trees such as pines, beeches, and magnolias. There are also some oddly named plants, such as tree daisies, milk trees, and cabbage trees. Among the plants live many species of birds, lizards, and insects.

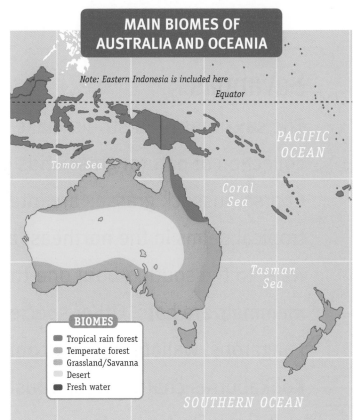

**MAIN BIOMES OF AUSTRALIA AND OCEANIA**

Note: Eastern Indonesia is included here

Equator

PACIFIC OCEAN

Timor Sea

Coral Sea

Tasman Sea

**BIOMES**
- Tropical rain forest
- Temperate forest
- Grassland/Savanna
- Desert
- Fresh water

SOUTHERN OCEAN

Red kangaroos can cover up to 25 feet (7.6 m) with each leap.

## Savannas

The savannas of Australia make up the largest collection of natural grasslands left on Earth. Coarse, tussock grasses are interrupted by tropical palms in the northeast and eucalyptus trees to the south. About one-third of savanna mammals are bats. Other species include kangaroos, wallabies, bandicoots, and possums. Kookaburras chatter in the brush, and wild black cockatoos feed on nuts and seeds.

# Rain Forests

Most tropical islands have thick rain forests. Papua New Guinea's rain forests cover about four-fifths of the country. They host more than 25,000 species of plants. Of the nation's 2,000 orchid species and 2,000 fern species, most are not found anywhere else on Earth. Additionally, more than 700 bird species live only in Papua New Guinea. Papuan rain forests are also home to rare tree kangaroos, birds of paradise, huge fruit bats, and tiny neon-green tree frogs.

Male twelve-wired birds-of-paradise are famous for their bright, colorful feathers.

# Oceans and Reefs

The Pacific Ocean is full of life. Coral reefs form where the ocean is clear, shallow, and at least 68 degrees Fahrenheit (20 degrees Celsius). Even if it might look like a plant, coral is actually an animal. It grows by producing coral **polyps**. Different types of coral live side by side on one reef. Pacific reefs shelter about 25 percent of all ocean life. The largest reef is the Great Barrier Reef, which stretches 1,400 miles (2,253 km) along northeastern Australia.

# Endangered Species

The environments of Australia and Oceania support many unusual animal species. However, some of these species are dying out. Without help, they could disappear forever.

## Northern Quoll

*Home: Australia*

The northern quoll is one of the few meat-eating marsupials. It is threatened by invasive cane toads. The toads are poisonous, and quolls die when they eat them. As cane toad populations increase, the threat to northern quolls increases.

## Kakapo

*Home: New Zealand*

The kakapo is a nearly flightless parrot that is easy prey for cats, dogs, and snakes. These predators did not live in New Zealand until Europeans began settling the islands. The birds once numbered in the thousands, but now only about 150 wild kakapos remain in two small locations.

## Long-Beaked Echidna

*Home: Papua New Guinea*

Humans are cutting down Papua New Guinea's forests and using the space to raise crops. The long-beaked echidna—a spiky, porcupine-like animal—is among the species losing their homes to deforestation.

## Giant Bumphead Parrotfish

*Home: Coral reefs in the Indian and Pacific oceans*

This 90-pound (41 kg) fish chews its way through coral reefs. One threat to the parrotfish is the nets of fishers. Another is the death of coral reefs, the parrotfish's food source.

# Ocean Acidification

Due to a process called acidification, the ocean waters of Oceania and Australia are in danger. Human activities such as operating cars, running factories, and burning coal release carbon dioxide. When carbon dioxide mixes with water, it creates carbonic acid. This acid threatens ocean life. Some animals, such as snails and clams, cannot grow the protective shells they need to survive in this acidic environment. Coral can no longer get chemicals it needs to grow strong reef support. In turn, animals that feed on shelled animals and coral can die from lack of food.

**Healthy coral**

# What happens?

- The ocean becomes more acidic.
- Shellfish cannot form shells.
- As coral reefs die, algae and jellyfish grow rapidly in numbers.
- The ocean food chain is thrown out of balance.

Dying coral at the Great Barrier Reef

Power plants that burn fossil fuels release dangerous chemicals into the air.

# What is the cause?

- Human activities produce carbon dioxide.
- Oceans absorb carbon dioxide from the air. The carbon dioxide dissolves in the water, forming carbonic acid.
- This process is happening about 100 times faster than the average rate over the past 55 million years.

# What can we do?

- Reduce fossil fuel use.
- Spread the word about pollution and acidification

Maori seafarers traveled in canoes with two hulls for safer ocean voyages.

Polynesian explorers sailed the Pacific Ocean in handmade boats.

# CHAPTER 3

# A Peek at the Past

People have lived in Australia for at least 65,000 years. Early Australian **Aboriginal** people lived in clans along the coasts and in the deserts. They hunted for meat and gathered fruits, nuts, and berries. Humans first arrived in Papua New Guinea about 50,000 years ago. Scientists found small, stone hand tools in an ancient settlement in the rain forest–covered mountains. No one can figure out how the tools were used.

Haʻamonga ʻa Maui is a stone structure that was built by the people of Tonga sometime in the 1200s CE.

## Settling the Islands

Much later, Polynesian settlers arrived on the many Pacific islands. They crossed the ocean from Asia by paddling canoes. Tonga's first settlers arrived between 1500 and 1000 BCE. Vanuatu and Samoa have been occupied for about 3,000 years. Polynesian settlers became the first Maori people in New Zealand in about 800 CE. These people all left behind tools, animal bones, and other artifacts that show when they arrived on the different islands of Oceania.

# Europeans Arrive

In the 1500s and 1600s, European explorers sought a quick route to Asia, where they often traded for goods such as silks and spices. In 1521, Spain's Ferdinand Magellan was the first explorer to visit many South Pacific islands. In 1568, Spanish captain Álvaro de Mendaña arrived in the Solomon Islands. In 1642, Dutch explorer Abel Tasman landed in what is now known as Tasmania. Within a year, Tasman also visited New Zealand, Tonga, and Fiji.

Ferdinand Magellan led the first expedition ever to sail around the entire world.

# British Control

Great Britain established a **colony** in Australia in 1788. Settlements in Sydney, Hobart, Brisbane, Adelaide, Melbourne, and Perth grew as more Europeans arrived. The discovery of gold in 1851 encouraged even more people to move to Australia. First came miners, then merchants to sell them goods. Tent cities sprang up, and men soon sent for their families.

# Timeline of Oceania Events

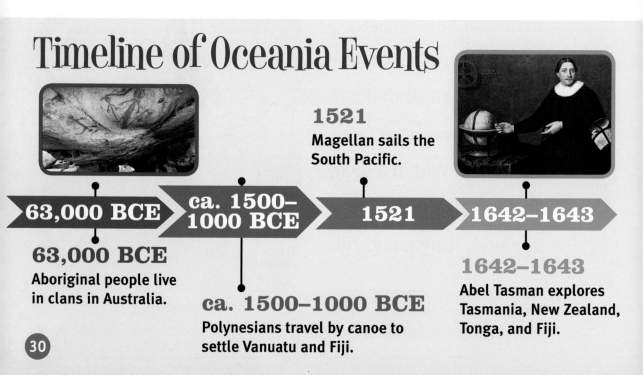

**1521**
Magellan sails the South Pacific.

**63,000 BCE** — **ca. 1500–1000 BCE** — **1521** — **1642–1643**

**63,000 BCE**
Aboriginal people live in clans in Australia.

**ca. 1500–1000 BCE**
Polynesians travel by canoe to settle Vanuatu and Fiji.

**1642–1643**
Abel Tasman explores Tasmania, New Zealand, Tonga, and Fiji.

By 1880, Australia's population had reached 2,231,231 people. New Zealand also became a British colony in 1840, followed by southern Papua New Guinea in 1884. Great Britain also set up colonies and **protectorates** in Fiji (1874), Kiribati (1892), the Solomon Islands (1893), and Tonga (1900). In the early 1900s, Great Britain handed off the responsibility for governing some of its Pacific territories to Australia and New Zealand.

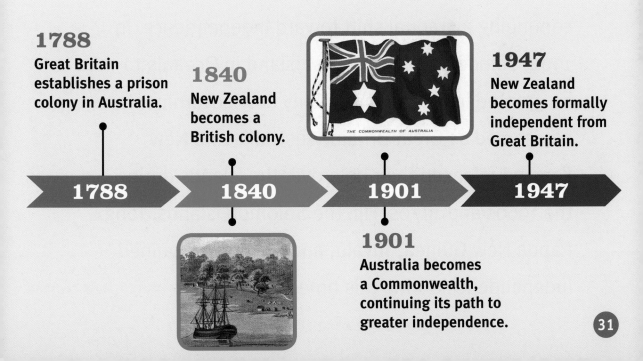

**1788**
Great Britain establishes a prison colony in Australia.

**1840**
New Zealand becomes a British colony.

**1947**
New Zealand becomes formally independent from Great Britain.

THE COMMONWEALTH OF AUSTRALIA

1788    1840    1901    1947

**1901**
Australia becomes a Commonwealth, continuing its path to greater independence.

# Seeking Independence

Australia became a **Commonwealth** in 1901, continuing a gradual shift toward independence. In 1962, Samoa became the first island in Oceania to be granted independence. Many new governments blossomed as Great Britain, Australia, and New Zealand released their hold over the islands during the 1960s and 1970s. Fiji, the Solomon Islands, Tonga, Papua New Guinea, Tuvalu, and Vanuatu all gained independence during this time.

# Dreaming Cave Paintings

For the Australian Aboriginal people, the Dreaming is a collection of stories and beliefs that explain the creation of the land, weather, animals, and plant life. Aboriginal people painted this picture of the Lightning Man in Australia's Kakadu National Park. In the Dreaming stories, the Lightning Man brings terrible rainstorms to the land. He also causes lightning strikes by striking trees with his mighty ax.

**THINK ABOUT IT:**
What can Dreaming stories tell us about the way early Aboriginal people saw the world?

Artwork such as this rock drawing of the Lightning Man is an important primary source for learning about the history of Australian Aboriginal people.

Maori warriors performed the haka war dance to scare their enemies—and it often worked!

The Maori All Blacks rugby team perform a traditional Maori haka before each game.

# CHAPTER 4

# The Continent Today

Although ocean waters separate the continent's countries, the islands of Australia and Oceania have many connections. The internet and cell phones link small islands to large landmasses and the rest of the world. Movies, satellite television, and computers have changed the lifestyles of local people. But even though they have modern cities, high-rise buildings, and busy seaports, most countries in Australia and Oceania have kept their unique character.

# Population

Australia and Oceania have a combined population of 41,183,198 people. This is about 0.54 percent of the world's population. Australia has the largest population, with more than 25 million people. Tuvalu has the fewest people, with only 11,052 residents. Seven out of 10 people in Australia and Oceania live in cities. Major cities include Sydney, Melbourne, Perth, and Brisbane in Australia. Wellington and Auckland are big cities in New Zealand. Port Moresby is the largest city in Papua New Guinea.

Auckland, New Zealand, is home to about 1.66 million people.

New Zealand politicians perform the *hongi*, a traditional Maori greeting where people press their foreheads and noses together.

# Governments

Governments vary among the countries of Australia and Oceania. However, they all have elections, heads of government, and **legislatures**. Some are **constitutional monarchies** with elected prime ministers. These countries include Australia, New Zealand, Tuvalu, and the Solomon Islands. The Marshall Islands have a two-house legislature, but it is not quite like the one in the United States. One chamber is elected and passes laws. The other is a purely advisory council of traditional high chiefs.

Ecotourism brings people to Australia to see incredible animals such as this great white shark.

# Economy

Many people of Oceania depend on fishing and farming to feed their families. The economies of some Oceania countries rely on tourists visiting white sand beaches. Today, the growing popularity of ecotourism is also helping the islands' economies grow. Ecotourism activities include whale watching, reef diving, and hiking through dense tropical forests.

Australia and New Zealand are tourist destinations, too. However, as developed economies, they also have other ways of making money. Both countries have factories, and they export wool, wheat, meat, processed foods, and minerals such as iron, copper, and gold.

# Processed in Australia and Oceania: Liquefied Natural Gas

Liquefied natural gas is a type of fossil fuel. It begins as a gas that is cooled to −260°F (−162°C) to make it liquid. Once it becomes a liquid, the fuel takes up 600 times less space than it did in gas form. This makes it easier to export to other countries. Australia is one of the world's top producers of liquefied natural gas. The sales of this fuel add more than $16 billion per year to the country's economy. Other countries on the continent that produce this valuable fuel include New Zealand and Papua New Guinea. The gas is exported to countries such as Japan, South Korea, and China.

The containers on this tanker ship at an Australian facility contain liquefied natural gas that is bound for Japan.

Fish head soup is a popular dinner in Oceania. Many people add rice to the leftovers and serve it for breakfast.

# Food and Fun

What's for dinner in Australia and Oceania? Each country has its own food traditions, but some dishes are popular across the continent. Coconuts grow wild throughout Oceania, making them a common, low-cost treat. Fish is essential. People catch it fresh, then use it to make soup, grill it, or even eat it raw.

In between meals, it is time for fun in the sun. Swimming, surfing, and fishing are popular sports. The era of British rule also introduced people to sports such as rugby and cricket. Australia also has its own unique style of football.

# Celebrations!

All of the region's cultures enjoy their own holidays and traditions. In many Oceanian cultures, naming a child takes place months after the child is born with a special ceremony. Island cultures each have their own unique forms of dance, food, and art. Many people receive elaborate tattoos to show that they have reached adulthood. Deaths are mourned with chanting and other traditions. Many cultures still practice these customs today, keeping their heritage alive.

Vanuatu's land divers leap from high towers to end up as close to the ground as possible. This act celebrates a boy's passage to manhood.

# Destination:

**DEI DEI HOT SPRINGS**
Papua New Guinea

Pools of mud bubble and belch. A geyser spews boiling water. Sneaky pitcher plants catch and eat buzzing flies. All this happens while visitors soak in the natural Dei Dei Hot Springs in Papua New Guinea.

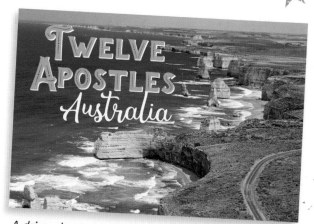

Micronesia

**CORAL REEFS IN CHUUK**

Diving into a coral reef like the ones in Chuuk is an eerie experience. Soft coral moves like a delicate fern, but it is actually an animal! An underwater camera is essential to capture the beauty of the reef and its dwellers.

**TENARU FALLS**
Solomon Islands

It is a long hike but well worth the effort to see the delicate Tenaru Falls in the Solomon Islands. This 200-foot (61 m), three-section waterfall is considered by tourists to be the best in the South Pacific.

**TWELVE APOSTLES**
Australia

A drive along the Great Ocean Road offers a view of the Twelve Apostles. These rock stacks were once part of the nearby cliffs. Years of wearing away from wind and water carved this remarkable scene.

# Australia and Oceania

Waitomo Caves are not studded with twinkling lights. That beautiful glow actually comes from thousands of glowworms hanging from the cave's roof! This species of glowworm lives only in New Zealand.

Talamahu Market is the place to go on a Saturday morning in Nuku'alofa, Tonga. Hand-carved wooden statues, taro root, pineapples, fresh fish—anything that someone might want is for sale at this street market. People looking for entertainment can also pick up a game of checkers with one of the stall owners.

At Tamaki Village, New Zealand's native people, the Maori, share their traditions, dress, language, and music. The village's warriors perform the haka, a dance done before battle to frighten enemies. Visitors share a hangi feast, which is cooked over a pit of hot stones.

Tasman Glacier Lake features icebergs floating in the water. The bergs calve off the local glacier, producing an unexpected sight in the South Pacific.

**Tallest peak:** Mount Wilhelm, Papua New Guinea, 14,793 ft. (4,509 m)

**Longest river:** Murray River, Australia, 1,570 mi. (2,527 km)

**Oldest city:** Sydney, Australia, 1788

**Country with the smallest population:** Tuvalu, 11,052

**Country with the largest population:** Australia, more than 25 million

**Number of different languages spoken in Papua New Guinea:** Nearly 850

**Highest recorded annual rainfall:** Bellenden Ker, Australia (2000), 490.5 in. (12.5 m)

## Did you find the truth?

**T** People have lived in Australia for about 60,000 years.

**F** All the islands of Oceania are volcanic islands.

# Resources

## Books

Bjorkland, Ruth. *Tasmanian Devils*. New York: Children's Press, 2013.

Friedman, Mel. *Australia and Oceania*. New York: Scholastic, 2009.

Gitlin, Marty. *Australia*. Minneapolis: Bellwether Media, 2018.

McClellan, Ray. *Maori Warriors*. Minneapolis: Bellwether Media, 2012.

Rector, Rebecca Kraft. *The Great Barrier Reef*. Mendota Heights, MN: North Star Editions, 2018.

Shepherd, Donna Walsh. *New Zealand*. New York: Children's Press, 2016.

**Visit this Scholastic website for more information on Australia and Oceania:**

★ www.factsfornow.scholastic.com

Enter the keywords **Australia and Oceania**

# Important Words

**Aboriginal** (ab-uh-RIJ-uh-nuhl) relating to the native people of Australia

**colony** (KAH-luh-nee) a territory that has been settled by people from another country and is controlled by that country

**commonwealth** (KAH-muhn-welth) a nation or state that is governed by the people who live there

**constitutional monarchies** (kahn-stih-TOO-shuh-nuhl MAH-nur-keez) governments with a king or queen whose powers are limited by a document that sets up how the government will run

**hemisphere** (HEM-ih-sfeer) one-half of a round object, especially of Earth

**legislatures** (LEJ-is-lay-churz) groups of people who have the power to make or change laws for a country or state

**marsupials** (mahr-SOO-pee-uhlz) any of a large group of animals that includes the kangaroo, the koala, and the opossum; female marsupials carry their babies in pouches on their abdomens

**plateaus** (plah-TOHZ) areas of level ground that are higher than the surrounding area

**polyps** (PAH-luhps) small sea animals with tubular bodies and round mouths surrounded by tentacles

**protectorates** (pruh-TEK-tuh-rits) countries that are run and protected by another larger country

# Index

Page numbers in **bold** indicate illustrations.

# About the Author

Barbara Somervill has written more than 250 books on many different topics. She was born and educated in New York and has lived in Canada, Australia, California, and South Carolina. She has one degree in English and another in library science. She loves to travel, read, color, and bake brownies.